The Deutsche Bibliothek holds
a record for this publication in the
Deutsche Nationalbibliografie;
detailed bibliographical data can
be found under http://dnb.ddb.de

Library of Congress Control
Number is available

©2011, Foster + Partners,
London, and Prestel Verlag,
Munich · London · New York

Prestel Verlag, A Member
of Verlagsgruppe Random
House GmbH

Prestel Verlag
Neumarkter Str. 28
81673 Munich
Germany
Tel   +49 (0)89 4136-0
Fax +49 (0)89 4136-2335
www.prestel.de

Prestel Publishing
900 Broadway, Suite 603
New York, NY 10003
USA
Tel +1 (212) 995-2720
Fax +1 (212) 995-2733

Prestel Publishing Ltd
4 Bloomsbury Place
London
WC1A 2QA
UK
Tel +44 (020) 7323-5004
Fax +44 (020) 7636-8004
www.prestel.com

ISBN 978-3-7913-4589-5

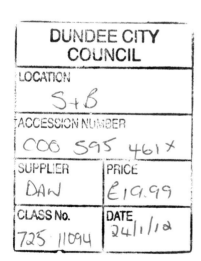

The Reichstag Foster + Partners

Norman Foster
Chris Abel

PRESTEL
MUNICH · LONDON · NEW YORK

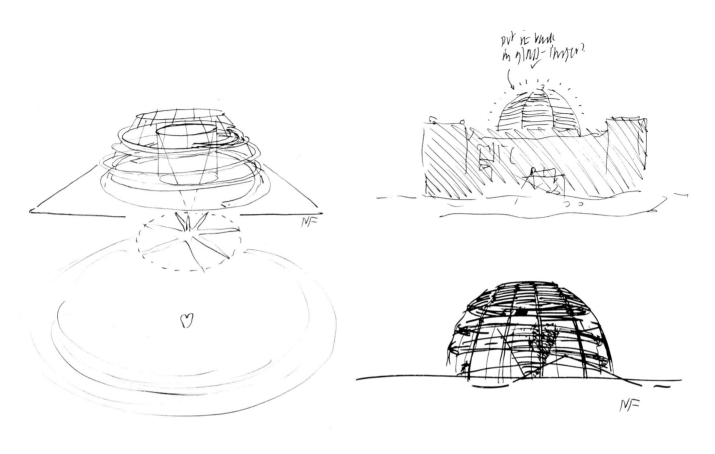

Norman Foster's early sketches explore the design of the cupola and its relationship with the roof terrace. One sketch, made on his first visit to the Reichstag in July 1992, was to prove prophetic; the note suggests of the dome: 'Put it back in glass – lighter?'

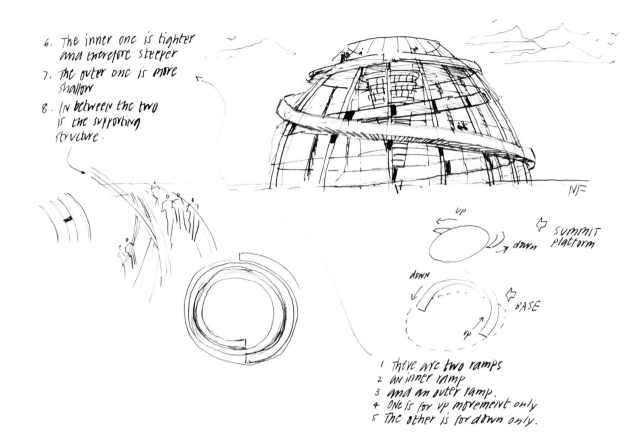

6. The inner one is tighter and therefore steeper

7. The outer one is more shallow

8. In between the two is the supporting structure.

UP

down

SUMMIT platform

DOWN

down

BASE

up

1. There are two ramps
2. an inner ramp
3. and an outer ramp.
4. One is for up movement only
5. The other is for down only.

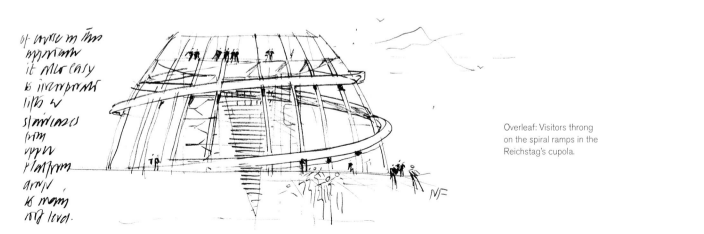

of course in this experience it also easy to interpret lifts w staircases from upper platform arriv to main roof level.

Overleaf: Visitors throng on the spiral ramps in the Reichstag's cupola.

5

Introduction Norman Foster

When, in April 1992, I received the letter from the President of the Bundestag that invited me, along with thirteen other architects from around the world, to enter an open competition to rebuild the Reichstag as the new home of the German parliament, I was honoured but sceptical. Could a foreign architect really be charged with a task of such significance, not only as a symbol of national identity but as a political institution and German presence on the world stage? I took the initiative of going to Bonn to share my concerns with the politicians and the organisers of the competition. I returned convinced that they were sincere in their intentions and that there was a genuine spirit of openness at the heart of the endeavour.

The 'openness' that I sensed on my visit forms a consistent theme throughout our project, allied with a number of related issues: the significance of the Bundestag as one of the world's great democratic forums; a commitment to making the parliament publicly accessible and its workings transparent; an understanding of history as a force that shapes buildings as well as the lives of nations; the integration of art and architecture; and a passionate commitment to a sustainable way of building.

My starting point was the belief that a parliament building should be physically open and inviting to the society it serves. I saw the inscription above the West Portico – *Dem Deutschen Volke* – as a signal for the future more than a reminder of the past. The results are radical. Where else in the world can politicians, citizens and visitors alike walk together through the main ceremonial entrance of their parliament building, rise to a public terrace on the roof, then follow ramps up to a viewing platform or share the same restaurant for a coffee or a meal?

The concept of reinventing the roof level as a public space was initially ridiculed by some MPs but was finally adopted as the result of our advocacy. In the process we pioneered a new kind of relationship between the public and the politicians, symbolically raising the citizens above the heads of those who represent them and are answerable to them. Light conditions permitting, from the roof and from the press lobby you can look down into the chamber and watch proceedings unfolding below.

Our first competition scheme responded to the fact that the Reichstag has formed the backdrop for almost every major public event in post-war Berlin, from rallies to rock concerts. We placed the Reichstag at the heart of a new public forum, sheltered beneath an oversailing roof 'umbrella' that symbolically unified old and new. This roof also worked ecologically, harvesting energy, reflecting daylight into the interiors and driving a system of natural ventilation. However, with the adoption of the Spreebogen masterplan for the government quarter, the brief for the second stage of the competition was reduced dramatically. Rather than try to adapt our scheme – as the other competitors did – we elected to begin again from scratch.

When I first visited the Reichstag, the only way in was at undercroft level, through a small doorway to the south – hardly an appropriate entrance to the nation's most important civic building. The reopening of the route up the grand flight of steps to the West Portico, which had been blanked off and its doors barred, was a result of our advocacy. Historical research gave further clues. We restored the original orientation of the chamber, which means that as you enter you look directly at the seats of the President of the Bundestag, the Chancellor and other national figures, and we reinstated the piano nobile as the main parliamentary level. In other significant ways, however, our approach represented a departure from the past. Originally the Reichstag was highly compartmentalised; the chamber itself took no account of the volume of the dome above. In contrast, we liberated the building spatially, slicing through it from top to bottom, drawing in light and opening up views.

Organisationally the building reflects a complex mix of public and private uses. Parliamentarians, public and press each have a place; sometimes they remain apart, in other instances their realms overlap. The press and members of the public may sit in the chamber to listen to debates. It was important for us that they should feel involved in that process. We designed the space so that it would encourage an intimate relationship between those in the public tribunes and speakers on the floor of the chamber.

Beyond the chamber are spaces that form part of the parliamentary machinery. A key consideration was to encourage activity within the building when parliament is not in session. We proposed that the faction rooms, or party meeting rooms, should not be segregated in neighbouring buildings, as they were in Bonn, but should be integrated within the Reichstag, an arrangement that has proved very popular with MPs.

The history of the building from its completion in 1894 to 1992 had been one of uncertainty and mutilation. After the Second World War, the remains of the dome had been removed and the facades 'restored', losing much of their ornament in the process. Inside, everything visible was entirely of the 1960s. What survived of the historic interiors had been concealed behind a lining of plasterboard and asbestos. Incredibly, when those layers were carefully stripped away, we found vivid imprints of the building's past – original mouldings, masons' marks and graffiti left by Russian soldiers in 1945. I argued that these fragments should be preserved: an approach that initially met with opposition from some quarters. Our philosophy prevailed and as a result the Reichstag now also functions as a 'living museum' of German history.

The element that perhaps expresses our radicalism most clearly is the cupola. When the question of a cupola was first discussed it was against a background of powerful voices clamouring for the historic dome to be reinstated. I was passionately opposed to that idea and refused to be a party to it. However, I was also enthusiastic about the idea of the Reichstag physically signalling its transformation on the Berlin skyline in some way. It was in that sense that I conceived the new cupola as a 'lantern' – a symbol of our quest to 'lighten' the spirit and mass of the old building.

Crucially, the cupola also forms a key component in the building's environmental strategy. At its core is a 'light sculptor', a mirrored cone that works like a lighthouse in reverse to direct daylight deep down into the chamber, while the sunshield that tracks around inside the cupola minimises solar gain and glare in summer, but admits the warmth of sunlight in winter.

The cone also plays a role in the chamber's natural ventilation system, extracting warm air at high level.

Germany has led the world in its environmental legislation, and from the outset our aim was to demonstrate in the Reichstag the potential for a wholly sustainable public building. I was alarmed to discover that the fossil-fuel powered services installed in the Reichstag in the 1960s emitted 7,000 tonnes of carbon dioxide every year; and heating the building over the same period consumed enough energy to warm 5,000 homes. In contrast, the building now derives its energy from renewable biofuel – refined vegetable oil from date palm, rape or sunflower seeds – which when burned in a co-generator to produce electricity is remarkably clean and efficient. As an illustration of how successful it is, heating and cooling the building today produces 440 tonnes of carbon dioxide annually – a 94 per cent reduction.

Surplus heat from the power plant is stored as warm water in a natural aquifer deep below ground and pumped back up when required to heat the building or to drive an absorption-cooling plant to produce chilled water. That too can be stored below ground and used in the summer to provide cooling via chilled ceilings. The building's energy demands have also been managed down. In fact they are modest enough to allow the Reichstag to perform effectively as a local power station. In that sense the project is a mini-manifesto for the cause of renewable energy.

While the initiatives I have described so far were ours as architects that was not always the case. One instance is the use of colour. My instinct was that a parliament building should have 'gravitas', which led to a palette of muted colours and natural materials. In the past we have used colour accents as a visual aid to navigating large, complex buildings. Our strategy at the Reichstag was to use colour to identify different floor levels or groups of activities. However, Chancellor Kohl challenged us: he believed that younger generations would want to see brighter, more colourful interiors. I also recognised that colour might help to moderate the building's monumental character and took the step of inviting the Danish artist Per Arnoldi to explore with us how a programme of colours might be developed for the public rooms. The blue of the seating in the chamber is particularly distinctive, as is the bright red in the rooftop restaurant.

As the project developed I worked closely with the many leading German and international artists who were commissioned to create works of art for specific locations in the building. Today the Reichstag is an extraordinary gallery of art, a repository of works that commemorate the contemporary creative spirit. Together they represent another, celebratory episode in the Reichstag's story.

The last major event in the life of the building before reconstruction work began was Christo and Jeanne-Claude's *Wrapped Reichstag*. The wrapping seemed to unburden the building of its tragic associations and prepare it for the next phase of its career. In that sense it was cathartic. Seeing the Reichstag sparkling in its silver shroud and witnessing the extraordinary festival that sprang up around it was an unforgettable experience.

Rebuilding the Reichstag became an all-consuming experience. It was a privilege to be entrusted with that task and, with my colleagues, to help to bring the Reichstag to its rebirth. That this process was followed through with complete openness, fairness and resolution speaks more about the qualities of German society than anything that I might say on the subject.

The Reichstag's vision of a public architecture that redresses the ecological balance, providing energy rather than consuming it, is an essential expression of optimism. It is also optimistic in another sense. As night falls and the cupola glows, lit from the chamber below, the building becomes a beacon, signalling the strength and vigour of the German democratic process.

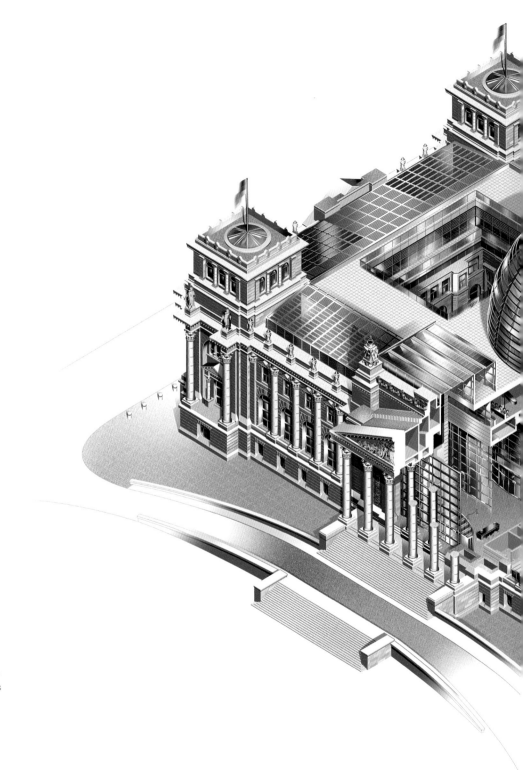

A cutaway drawing showing how the chamber and cupola have been inserted within the existing masonry shell. Public access is via the West Portico – a route that historically was used only for state occasions. Lifts take visitors either to the public tribunes in the chamber, or to the roof terrace and the cupola.

Rebuilding the Reichstag Chris Abel

Most architectural history is bad history. Buildings and styles come and go almost in a world of their own, their historians too intent on cataloguing their formal and spatial attributes to pay much attention to the larger political and social events which ultimately lend them meaning, and frequently change it.

The Reichstag in Berlin is a building that defies the conventional narrow focus, compelling historian and critic alike to reverse their normal approach in favour of a broader perspective. A ponderous, Neoclassical confection, with a workable plan but no other special merit in itself, the original building designed by Paul Wallot in the nineteenth century has been overwhelmed by historic events of such magnitude as to render any normal physical or spatial description practically redundant. More perhaps than any other building in modern times, the Reichstag is significant not for its architecture per se, but for what it has absorbed and tells us of the great events it has witnessed.

As a student of architecture at the Hochschule für Bildende Künste (HfBK) in West Berlin in 1960-62, the transformation of the Reichstag from war-damaged shell to the new home of the German Parliament carries a special meaning for this writer. Lured to the city initially on a summer vacation in search of some

of Modernism's greatest works, the idea of Berlin then in mind was mostly shaped by cinematic images of bombed-out ruins haunted by leather-coated spies.

The first sight of the sunny pavement cafés along the Kurfürstendamm – or Ku'damm as it is called – was therefore something of a surprise. Created to rival Paris' Champs-Elysées, it represented a pre-war quality of urban life one presumed had been either bombed or strangled into extinction. Staying temporarily in the outlying district of Wannsee, in the midst of the forests and lakes that surround the city, it became clear how West Berliners managed to survive living year-in, year-out imprisoned within the city limits. Communist East Germany – the German Democratic Republic (GDR) – then completely encircled the western part of the city, save for two closely guarded land corridors, one to the west and one to the south, through which suitably documented individuals and goods were allowed to pass.

In 1960 there was still no Berlin Wall – that went up the following summer – but the change from East to West was dramatic enough. The Brandenburg Gate, an eighteenth-century triumphal arch marking the edge of the Tiergarten and the beginning of the broad avenue of Unter den Linden, was then one of the busiest checkpoints between the two parts of the city, along

Left: The inscription *Dem Deutschen Volke* is attached to the West Portico in 1916. The bronze letters were cast from Napoleonic cannon captured at the Battle of Leipzig a century earlier.

Opposite: The Reichstag and Königsplatz depicted in nineteenth- and early twentieth-century postcards.

Above: The west front of the newly completed Reichstag, seen in 1898. The building was intended to embody the might and unity of the German Empire, although it was scorned by the Kaiser as the *Reichsaffenhaus* – 'Imperial ape house'. Another contemporary critic described it as 'a first-class hearse'.

Above: A cross-section through the assembly chamber and dome as completed by Paul Wallot; he wrote: 'The building is primarily intended for practical use and the design reflects this'. Nonetheless, with an enclosed volume of 400,000 cubic metres it provided only 12,000 square metres of usable floor space.

with the U-Bahn and S-Bahn stations situated near the border. East Berliners working in the West or visiting relatives and friends there would cross daily in their thousands, showing their identity cards to the border guards as they did so. Most returned at the end of the day but increasing numbers chose not to, joining the swelling stream of refugees from other parts of East Germany passing through Berlin's relatively open borders.

Just inside the Tiergarten and a couple of hundred metres to the north of the Brandenburg Gate on Königsplatz, close to the River Spree, stood the pockmarked hulk of the Reichstag, surrounded by a treeless parkland flattened in the final Russian assault in 1945. Enrolled as part of Berlin's inner defences, the Reichstag fell under direct bombardment before succumbing to Russian infantry on 1 May. Miraculously, after the war, although denuded of most of its ornamentation and statuary, the main structure remained virtually intact. In the following years, under the Four Power Agreement, the Reichstag fell into the orbit of the British occupying forces, which controlled that part of the city. Left untouched until the early 1960s, it stood as a grim reminder of German defeat, signalling the transition from West to East and still worse conditions over the border.

Beyond the Brandenburg Gate and along Unter den Linden, once the fashionable centre of pre-war Berlin, lay the bleak International Style offices and apartment blocks, which were the GDR's fragile claim to modernity and equality with the West. Interspersed by the remaining monuments to former glories, such as Karl Friedrich Schinkel's Schauspielhaus and Altes Museum, the widely spaced towers and slabs and empty oversized 'plazas', represented orthodox Modernism's worst failings. Still further east was Alexanderplatz, rebuilt in the same fashion, and the ominous, Soviet-style buildings of Stalin-Allee – since renamed Karl-Marx-Allee – while everywhere laid the sad ruins and cleared building sites of a still devastated city. Only when one journeyed out to the green fringes of East Berlin could one find again the same relief as one found in the West.

By 1961 the number of East German refugees exiting through Berlin had risen to nearly 4.5 million, driving the frustrated GDR government to cut off the flow completely. Hastily erected overnight on 12-13 August, and reinforced over the next few months, the immediate effect of the Berlin Wall on both sides of the city and its population was traumatic: socially, psychologically and politically. The repercussions were immediate, threatening to spill over into global conflict.

17

Left: The Reichstag in flames on the night of 27 February 1933. The Nazis claimed that the fire was the start of a left-wing uprising and used it as a pretext to arrest prominent Communists.

They rose to a dangerous peak in a stand-off between American and Russian tanks across 'Checkpoint Charlie' on Friedrichstrasse on 25 October – watched apprehensively on the spot by this writer – presaging the Cuban Missile Crisis of the following year.

Later, with the immediate political crisis over, attention turned to more subtle forms of response. Architecture had already found a place as a cultural weapon in post-war Berlin with the 1955-57 *Interbau*, or permanent housing exhibition in the Hansaviertel, a Modernist development laid out strictly according to CIAM principles. Standing in parkland and designed by a host of foreign and local luminaries such as Walter Gropius, Arne Jacobsen, Oscar Niemeyer and Egon Eiermann, its mixture of high- and low-rise buildings was infinitely superior to anything to be found in the East.

By 1961 Hans Scharoun's Philharmonie was also under construction on Potsdamer Strasse not far from the border, becoming the first component of the Kulturforum, an arts complex intended to confirm West Berlin's cultural supremacy. In 1962 Mies van der Rohe was commissioned to design the New National Gallery on a site just a short distance away from the Philharmonie. Other, less celebrated new buildings also played their part in the propaganda war. Axel

Springer, a ferociously anti-Communist Berlin newspaper magnate, built his new headquarters tower hard against the Wall in a visible gesture of defiance. Whether great or indifferent in quality, architecture in West Berlin after the Wall took on all the well-aimed purpose of heavy artillery.

In addition to its ultra-sensitive location on the 'front line' – the Wall ran immediately behind the building – the Reichstag's symbolic status as the home of Germany's first democratic assembly automatically placed it in the forefront of these events, challenging commentators to confront its many meanings. Best known outside Germany for the infamous fire of 27 February 1933, which gave Adolf Hitler the pretext for assuming dictatorial powers, the history of the Reichstag has been imbued with contradiction and myth almost from its very inception.

The political credentials of the building and its occupants were always ambiguous. In 1871, when the first architectural competition was held, most of the elected members of the Reichstag – themselves drawn from the upper strata of society – favoured designs that symbolised German imperial power. Delays in securing the site resulted in a second more limited competition ten years later, and Paul Wallot's winning scheme eventually gave them what they wanted.

Right: A postcard produced in the early years of the Nazi era, showing the Kroll Opera on Königsplatz, where the Reichstag was convened following the fire of 1933.

Left: Yevgeny Khaldei's celebrated photograph of the Red Flag being raised on the roof of the Reichstag; the scene was restaged for the camera on 2 May 1945, the flag having first been raised the evening before.

On signposts, on tanks, on shells for the guns, on gun barrels, there was only one message, painted in red: 'To the Reichstag!' Yelena Rzhevskaya, quoted in *How Wars End: Eye-witness Accounts of the Fall of Berlin*, 1969

Above: The Reichstag in ruins. On 2 May 1945 Soviet troops finally captured the Reichstag after a bloody battle that lasted four days. Inevitably associated with the Nazi suppression of the Communists, the Reichstag was a symbolic objective for Stalin and became the focus of the last major battle of the war in Europe.

Significantly, both Kaiser Wilhelm II, who presided over the building's completion, and Hitler who rendered it redundant, viewed the Reichstag's architecture with contempt and the institution it housed as a threat to their own interests. The Kaiser retained most of the real political power in his own hands until the end of the First World War and only belatedly agreed to the Reichstag's inscription, *Dem Deutschen Volke*, which was added in 1916 to appease popular disaffection with the war. And contrary to myth, Hitler himself never spoke there.

After the fire the Nazis convened the Reichstag assembly in the Kroll Opera, situated on the opposite side of Königsplatz. As for the Reichstag itself, it was destined in the Nazi scheme of things to be converted into a Parliamentary Library, an insignificant part of Hitler and Albert Speer's grandiose plans for the rebuilding of Berlin as Germania. Physically and symbolically dwarfed by Speer's inflated centrepiece, the domed Grosse Halle, an assembly building for 180,000 people, the Reichstag was to be stripped of its original purpose and meaning.

For Stalin and the Russian soldiers attacking the Reichstag in the last days of the war, however, the building remained a potent symbol both of German aggression and anti-Communist oppression. Directly or indirectly, from the failed 'German Revolution' in 1919, when the Social Democrats narrowly defeated an armed Communist uprising, followed by the Nazi persecution of the Communists after the Reichstag fire, through to Germany's invasion of the Soviet Union itself, the building became a focal point of opposition to Communist ambitions and a crucible for anti-German emotions. Victorious at last, Russian officers and soldiers thronged to the building to leave their mark on its columns and walls in dense graffiti, celebrating the moment of capture and their own hard journeys in reaching that point.

The eventual process of renovating the building got off to a faltering start. In 1954 the fragile remnants of the dome's iron framework were demolished to clear the way for work to begin. Not until three years later, however, did the Bundestag finally decide to proceed with the rebuilding, appointing a panel of architects including Hans Scharoun to draw up plans for its restoration. In 1959 a further decision was made to restore the Reichstag as a temporary seat of the German Bundestag, even though the Four Power status and occupation of Berlin meant that such a plan could not be implemented in the foreseeable future. The following year, in yet another gesture of optimism – only months before the erection of the Wall – an

architectural competition was held in preparation for the anticipated return of the German parliament to its historical home.

The winner of the competition was the Berlin architect Paul Baumgarten, a respected Modernist and teacher of the orthodox school, and a participant in the Hansaviertel *Interbau*. Baumgarten focused on rebuilding the parliamentary chamber and supporting functions along strictly contemporary lines, demolishing or concealing large sections of the original structure in the process. In the same 'modernising' spirit, Scharoun and his panel had earlier decided against rebuilding the dome. However, the four corner towers – which had served as anti-aircraft gun emplacements during the war – were restored, albeit reduced in height. Prevented from being used as intended, from 1971 the rebuilt Reichstag, bereft of its dome and its historical interiors, served mainly to house a permanent exhibition, *Fragen an die Deutsche Geschichte* – 'Questions on German History' – along with conferences and similar public functions.

The sudden and historic collapse in 1989 of the GDR along with Communist regimes throughout Eastern Europe, accompanied by the gleeful tearing down of the Berlin Wall in November that year by ecstatic Berliners from both sides, brought the

Reichstag's long hibernation to a dramatic close. Unexpectedly, dream became reality. On 4 October 1990, more than half a century after the building had witnessed its last full session, the Bundestag met in the Reichstag in celebration of German unity. The occasion was followed a little over two months later by a meeting of the first freely elected parliament of the reunified Germany.

In 1991 the Bundestag confirmed Berlin as the new capital and the Reichstag as its new home. Much as it had been anticipated, the decision finally to move to Berlin was not an easy one. Established in Bonn since 1950, the Bundestag and its members were then preparing to move into a brand new building in the city, designed by the German architect Günther Behnisch. Passed by a narrow majority – and only then after a passionately argued debate – the vote to move to Berlin rendered Behnisch's new building redundant before it was even completed.

In hindsight, the decision was inevitable. Strategically situated close to the frontier between Western and Eastern Europe, as Germany's historical capital Berlin had served as a vital link between both worlds, and was clearly destined to do so again. The Reichstag itself, though far from an ideal building as such, had also become so central to German history

Above: A view of the first
competition model; the Reichstag
and its oversailing canopy are
seen from the north bank of
the River Spree.

Right: One of a series of early
planning sketches by Norman
Foster.

Far right: A plan view of the
model of the first competition
scheme: the Reichstag was to be
hollowed out within its walls and
a 'house within a house' inserted.

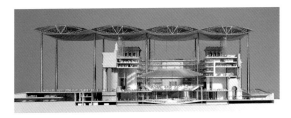

Left: A 1:200-scale sectional model of the first competition scheme, looking into the chamber. The Reichstag formed the centrepiece of a new public forum and the focus of a city quarter whose social life would have complemented the political activity within.

as to make any other choice of location in the city completely unthinkable.

In April 1992 an architectural competition for rebuilding the Reichstag ensued – the fourth in the building's history – open to all German architects and fourteen invited foreign practices. In the event, eighty German firms competed for a project many doubtless viewed with trepidation, given the Reichstag's chequered history. In January 1993, in a still more surprising outcome, the first prize was shared by three foreign architects: Norman Foster from the UK, Pi de Bruijn from the Netherlands and Santiago Calatrava from Spain, whose practice is based in Switzerland.

A subsequent run-off between the three finalists five months later was based on a new brief and left Foster as the clear winner. Remarkably, not only had Germany handed responsibility for its most sensitive architectural project of the century to an outsider, but it had chosen an architect from a former victorious and occupying country. Intentionally or not, the new German Parliament had added an extraordinary gesture of reconciliation to its growing record of achievement.

The Foster team's winning scheme was formulated in response to four main issues, which Foster has summarised as: 'a belief in the significance of the Bundestag as one of the great democratic forums of the world; making the process of government more accessible to the public; an understanding of history as a force which shapes buildings as well as the life of nations; and a passionate commitment to the low-energy, sustainable agenda which is fundamental to the architecture of the future'.

While the last of these issues is by now among the most familiar of the Foster studio's concerns, it acquires a special meaning in the German context, not just for the Reichstag project, but for German politics and society as a whole. Beginning with Chancellor Willy Brandt's 1969 commitment to the protection of nature and the countryside, environmental issues and politics have been inextricably connected in Germany, more so possibly than in any other country in the world. The related success of the German Green party and its eventual election into the Bundestag in the early 1980s confirmed the movement's entrenchment in official political life. Since then, much of the Green movement's agenda has been adopted by the main political parties, during which time Germany has become the environmental trailblazer in Europe.

Prior to the Reichstag competition Foster and his colleagues had had positive first-hand experience of German sensitivity to these issues in developing low-energy designs for the Microelectronic Park in

Right: This sketch by Norman Foster envisages galleries and cafés lining the south bank of the Spree, which would be opened up to the public for the first time.

Duisburg, completed in 1993, and the Commerzbank Headquarters in Frankfurt – the first truly 'green' tower – designed in 1991 and completed six years later. German architects Mark Braun and Stefan Behling, both of whom worked on the Reichstag, joined the design team during the same period, strengthening the practice's operations in the country. Foster's environmental approach to the Reichstag therefore not only reflected the practice's core values, but was an appropriate response to deeply held German social and political commitments.

The same might also be said for Foster's respect for the German parliamentary system. Accustomed as they are to think of Westminster as the 'mother of parliaments', many Britons would not share Foster's sentiments. There are, however, good reasons for Foster's assessment of the Bundestag and its related democratic institutions, which operate in a way quite unlike Westminster.

In contrast to the adversarial organisation and political customs that typify Westminster, the political structures of the German Federal Republic were designed to generate consensus. The keys to the way politics works in Germany are: 'institutional interdependence'; the dispersion of power; and the idea of the 'Rechtstaat', or a state based on the rule of law – all features given special prominence following the Nazi experience. The directly elected Bundestag itself is only part of a carefully balanced, bicameral system of legislature and mainly serves as a 'control function', examining and passing proposed changes to existing laws and regulations. These may emanate from any one of a number of sources: from the second chamber or Bundesrat, which represents the interests of the different Länder or regional states, from various semi-permanent bodies and ad hoc working committees, or from the civil service.

Since the Bundesrat and the other bodies and committees are comprised of MPs from all parties, the 'opposition' therefore plays an important role in the day-to-day functioning of government, making it possible for even small parties such as the Greens to initiate new legislation. Again, in contrast to Westminster, the dispersion of power in the Federal Republic was enshrined in a written constitution (the Basic Law of 1949) and reinforced by an electoral system that ensured a fair distribution of votes: coalition government and compromise has since been the norm in Germany rather than the exception.

Having experienced the loss of democracy under the Nazis, since 1945 the German people have therefore gone from the most extreme form

Left: In the second stage of the competition, Norman Foster presented four 'variations on a theme', ranging from modest rebuilding to full-scale renovation. In the chosen proposal shown here, the Reichstag's courtyards were retained and the raised roof element was reduced to a single pillow above the chamber.

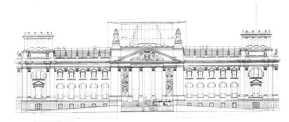
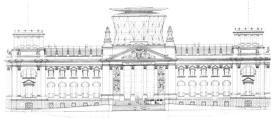

of authoritarian government to a system of broadly shared leadership of the state. Moreover, contrary to Anglo-Saxon criticisms of coalition government, the German system has a remarkably stable post-war record. The need to give expression to this open, transparent democratic system directly shaped Foster's approach to the Reichstag project in all its stages.

Amid all the public and professional acclaim for the final built design it is often forgotten that Foster initially resisted the idea of rebuilding the Reichstag's dome in any shape or form and openly declared himself against its reinstatement in replica. Like Baumgarten before him, Foster viewed the lost dome as an unnecessary and inappropriate symbol of centralised authority.

The scheme that the Foster team – led by Foster and his partner David Nelson – submitted for the first stage of the competition represented a radical departure. A great double-skinned roof canopy oversailed the old building, supported by twenty tapering, stainless steel columns. The result, when looking at the old building beneath it, was to emphasise the four corner towers, which Wallot had designed to symbolise the four major regional states of the first German Federation, expressing the decentralisation of power rather than its concentration.

The brief at this stage specified 33,000 square metres of usable space, far more than could be included within the original structure. Foster accommodated half this space, which was made up of committee rooms, administrative and subsidiary functions, in a podium that wrapped around all four sides of the building. Reaching right out to the banks of the Spree, the edge of the podium at this point followed the curve of the river, providing cafés, restaurants and other public amenities along a new river walk, all sheltered beneath the roof canopy.

Throughout the Reichstag's history – even when it lay in ruins – the space in front of the building has been the focus for public gatherings of all kinds, from political demonstrations to open-air concerts. Foster's first scheme celebrated this tradition. Also conceived as a unifying element in the composition, the roof provided protection for public events to take place on the new podium-level 'piazza', covering both the original building and its new extensions. A public ambulatory, running around the assembly chamber at piazza level, connected this exterior space to the interior, providing views of the activities within. Extending this theme, the roof of the Reichstag itself was also made accessible, literally and metaphorically lifting the public above their political representatives.

Above left: As the scheme developed, alternative solutions were explored for the treatment of the roof, introducing the idea of a raised viewing platform.

Above right: The conical reflector first appeared at the heart of a 'lighthouse', which would have provided a powerful marker on the skyline.

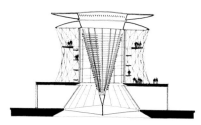

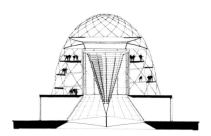

The visual effect of the spreading 'umbrella' roof, together with the concept of liberal public access, was to reinforce the symbolic dispersion of power, already represented by the four corner towers. In a further gesture, one of the corner roof columns was planted in the waters of the Spree, symbolically bridging the former dividing line between East and West.

In addition to the roof's protective and symbolic functions, it had a clearly delineated environmental role, each component in turn playing more than one part in an integrated system of climate control. As well as supporting the roof, the tapered hollow columns formed flues to provide a system of natural 'stack' ventilation for the spaces below. The upper surface of the roof itself was to be equipped with sufficient photovoltaic cells to make the building virtually self-sufficient in energy. Each pillow-shaped roof section also contained skylights to allow diffused natural light to penetrate the spaces below, while rainwater collected from the roof was to be utilised as 'grey' water in the building's other services.

However, events contrived to force Foster to drop this scheme in favour of a quite different and ultimately more modest approach. In parallel with the first Reichstag competition, another major competition was being held for the masterplan of the new government quarter, immediately to the north of the Reichstag in the Spreebogen, an area created by the loop in the Spree. As a result of that competition, which was won by the Berlin architects Axel Schultes and Charlotte Frank, it was decided that many of the ancillary functions of the Bundestag – most of which Foster had included within the podium – should instead be contained within the Spreebogen buildings.

The result was a drastic reduction – almost 60 per cent – in the total amount of floor space designated for the Reichstag project. During that same period, Germany was also going through a severe economic recession, partly brought about by the enormous costs of reunification and related development programmes in the former GDR, with the result that budgets as well as programmes were being scaled back. When it came to the eventual run-off between the three finalists, Foster – unlike his two rivals, who stuck to their original schemes – concluded that the changes to the brief required a fresh look at the entire project.

While the democratic and environmental aspects of the programme remained vital to the new scheme, the reduction in the brief compelled Foster to rethink his approach. With its public open 'forum' and waterfront amenities, the first scheme would have had a considerable impact on the surrounding area.

Right: The new rooftop feature – not yet a 'dome' – grew from Foster's conviction that the Reichstag should signal its transformation on the skyline. Its form progressed through a series of models and culminated in two alternatives: a structure known as the 'lighthouse' and a cupola, initially with a truncated top.

This larger, urban dimension of the project had now to be abandoned, the focus shifting instead to rebuilding within the Reichstag's original walls.

However, this decision posed special problems of its own. Little of the Reichstag's original volume of 400,000 cubic metres – the largest building of its time in Berlin – was ever usable. Of this, as much as 130,000 cubic metres comprised solid masonry or voids, while only 12,000 cubic metres performed as functional space. Baumgarten's renovations had only slightly modified this equation – hardly the most promising ground for an architecture of transparency, so central to the whole project!

Foster's second-stage submission showed a greatly altered scheme with the umbrella canopy gone and the plenary chamber capped instead by one of the original pillow-shaped modules. Nonetheless, important features from the first scheme survived, including open access to the roof level, where the public retained their 'dominant' symbolic status. Based on the team's research into the complexities of the German parliamentary process, they argued for some of the supporting political activities of the Bundestag, notably meeting rooms for the different parties, or 'factions', and facilities for the press lobby to be retained within the brief, and the scheme reflected that. Such mastery

of the inner workings of parliament earned the architects the respect of the members of the Building Committee and ultimately helped to secure their overwhelming support.

However, one question remained: the dome. Foster remained adamantly opposed to any idea of restoring the Reichstag's original dome. He even went on record to say that if a reconstruction of the historical dome was what the Building Committee wanted then someone else should do it. But over the next few months he and his colleagues came under increasing political and public pressure in both Bonn and Berlin to include a new roof feature of some kind in the scheme.

The ultimate design of what Foster calls the 'cupola' represents both a triumph of compromise – an appropriate result in itself for a political institution based on principles of negotiation – and the product of a subtle game in which both architect and client ultimately got what they wanted. For a practice all too frequently miscast as being interested only in technology, the handling of the symbolic dimensions of the dome's design – as with the treatment of the Reichstag's symbolism generally – also reveals new levels of complexity in Foster and his team's approach.

Foster's strategy for the 'reinvention' of the dome, and the reconstruction of the Reichstag as a whole

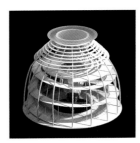
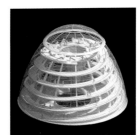

from the second stage of the competition, differs
completely from Baumgarten's. While Baumgarten's
orthodox Modernist intervention effectively displaced
or downgraded the older fabric and architecture, Foster
and his team favoured the creative interplay between
old and new, which neither pandered to the past nor
rejected it but created a new relationship from mutual
respect and dialogue.

This philosophy was first explored by the practice
in the mid-1980s, in a different context, in the subtle
relationship between the Carré d'Art, in Nîmes, and
the Maison Carrée, a finely preserved Roman temple
in the centre of the city. Situated immediately facing
the temple, the Carré d'Art is also conceived as a
free-standing pavilion structure and has its own portico.
While the proportions of the latter echo those of the
side elevation of the Roman structure, in other respects
they could hardly be more different. Both perfect
expressions of their own time, the two forms of
architecture and technology play against each other
so that each highlights the distinct qualities of its
opposite number to mutual benefit.

A closer precedent, however, though tiny in scale
compared with the Reichstag, is the Sackler Galleries
at the Royal Academy of Arts in London, completed in
1991, which Foster showed to visiting members of the

Reichstag Building Committee. Where the Maison
Carrée is a completely separate work, the Sackler
Galleries involved meshing together two equally
different forms of architecture in the same building
complex. Opening up views of the hitherto concealed
eighteenth-century facade of Burlington House and
the Victorian elevation of the galleries behind, Foster
inserted a new steel and glass stairway and lift in the
narrow light-well between the two blocks. The
Palladian and Victorian facades now face each other
across an elegant space shaped by modern design and
technology. A similar strategy guided Foster's scheme
for the Great Court at the British Museum, which was
begun in 1994 while detail design proceeded in Berlin.

In creating room for a larger assembly chamber
and adjacent reception hall, Baumgarten had gutted
much of the Reichstag's original central structure.
Having in turn stripped out Baumgarten's work –
including all the panelling and plaster linings, much
of which incorporated toxic asbestos – Foster took
advantage of the full width of the space left between
the walls of the Reichstag's two courtyards to create
a still larger assembly chamber. However, where
Baumgarten's interventions had obliterated any traces
of the building's original character, Foster's strategy
was to retain the surviving nineteenth-century fabric,

so that, as in the Sackler Galleries and the British Museum, clean lines and clear glass play directly against ornament and solid stone. The interplay between old and new is most apparent in the design of the glass-walled assembly chamber and in the surrounding lobby spaces, where the texture of the surviving stonework is most evident, including battle scars and Russian graffiti.

The assembly chamber itself involved much deliberation concerning an appropriate democratic form. Wallot's original chamber was based on the classic semi-circular plan favoured by most democratic political assemblies, including the United States Congress, which emphasises the unity and egalitarian nature of the gathering. Baumgarten's chamber was self-consciously designed to break with precedent and had a 'U' shaped configuration (Baumgarten also reversed the orientation of the chamber – an arbitrary change which was corrected in the Foster plan) – while Behnisch's Bonn chamber had a design based on a full circle. The circular plan stresses the unity of the assembly even more clearly but has the disadvantage of placing some members behind the seat of the Bundestag President.

In Foster's first competition scheme, the Reichstag chamber followed a circular seating arrangement similar to Behnisch's. For the final design, however, the team developed a compressed semi-circular layout – an arrangement that retains the democratic qualities of the classic seating plan but makes it easier for anyone to address a full gathering from the front. In keeping with tradition, Foster also placed his own three-dimensional version of the Federal German eagle in its traditional position behind the President.

Movement systems and space planning are also carefully designed to maintain security while ensuring maximum transparency. Public and politicians share the same entrance to the building, through the West Portico, from where the whole chamber and its occupants are clearly visible. Each goes their separate ways thereafter, though with much overlapping and interpenetrating of vertical spaces and sightlines, so that both public and parliamentarians are constantly aware of one another. Using their own lift or staircase, visitors with prior clearance may stop off at the mezzanine level, where they can take their seats alongside members of the press in the tribunes, which overlook proceedings in the chamber. However, most members of the public will go directly to the roof terrace, where they can dine in the restaurant, or promenade on the roof and in the cupola, enjoying the spectacular views across Berlin.

Above left: To assess the efficacy of the cone as a light reflector, a 1:20-scale model of the cupola and chamber was built and hoisted on to the roof of the Reichstag, where it could be tested in real light conditions.

Above right: Standing inside the model, from left: David Nelson, lighting designer Claude Engle, and Norman Foster.

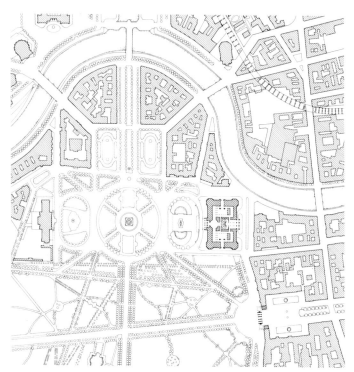

1901

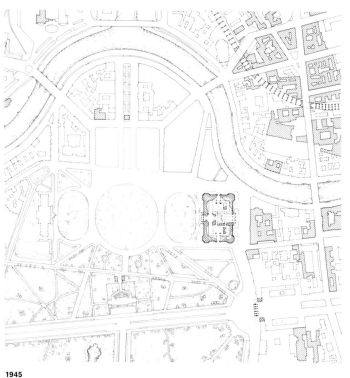

1945

Above left: A plan of Königsplatz and the Reichstag in 1901, when the Bismarck memorial was erected. The memorial and the Victory Column, or *Siegessäule*, were relocated to the Tiergarten in 1938.

Above right: A plan of the newly renamed Platz der Republik and the Reichstag in 1945; the scene of some of the most ferocious fighting in the Battle of Berlin, the square and the surrounding area lie in ruins.

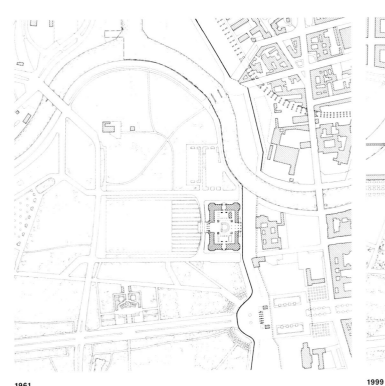

1961

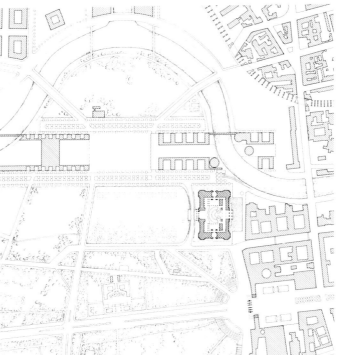

1999

Above left: The Platz der Republik and the Reichstag in 1961, seen after the erection of the Berlin Wall, which cut the city in two; the Wall ran close to the east front of the Reichstag, making the building inaccessible from that point.

Above right: The Platz der Republik and the Reichstag in 1999. The bar-like Spreebogen masterplan by Schultes-Frank, adopted in February 1993, was a crucial factor in Norman Foster's decision to rethink his 'big roof' proposals from first principles.

Below: The Reichstag relies extensively on daylight, solar energy and natural ventilation and makes use of renewable biofuel. The cone in the cupola reflects daylight into the chamber, while a sunshade blocks solar gain and glare. Biofuel is burned in a co-generator to produce heat and power. The surplus energy produced, in the form of hot water, drives an absorption cooling plant to produce chilled water. Excess hot and cold water are stored in natural aquifers, respectively 300 and 60 metres below ground.

Members of Parliament, on the other hand, have the first floor – or piano nobile – at entrance level to themselves. Here they have access to the floor of the plenary chamber and a variety of formal and informal meeting rooms, restaurants and bars, together with a multi-denominational chapel. The second floor is mostly taken up by administrative functions, the offices of the Bundestag President, the Council of Elders and formal reception rooms. A new third floor level created behind Wallot's original parapet contains the faction rooms and the press lobby and bar. These are grouped around a glazed, circular viewing gallery that forms the soffit of the chamber. The ground floor is mostly given over to maintenance functions, plant rooms and storage. Some amenities are also purposely designed to allow parliamentarians and visitors to mingle more freely, as in the press lobby bar and in the rooftop restaurant, both of which are regularly used by MPs.

The result is an intricate layering and intermeshing of public and semi-private realms which maintains public access without sacrificing security or hindering the smooth workings of the parliament. In a departure from the practice's normal preference for monochrome and subtle shades, different rooms and spaces are also picked out in a bright colour scheme. Foster originally proposed that the use of colour be restricted to a

Combined heat and power plant

Absorption cooling plant

Heat pump

Electrical power

Heating

Refined vegetable oil

coded system for doors to differentiate between floors and aid visitor orientation, much as the studio has used colour in the past. However, Chancellor Helmut Kohl argued persuasively for a brighter, more youthful palette in the Reichstag.

Warming to the idea, Foster asked the Danish artist Per Arnoldi – with whom he also collaborated on the colour scheme for the Commerzbank – to help develop a broader palette. The scheme they devised includes the colour coding of the doors, floor by floor, but also provides each major room with its own colour signature. In the same spirit, the seating in the chamber is upholstered in what is now known as 'Reichstag blue'. The colour brings out the full shape of the assembly and differentiates it from the grey seating in the public and press galleries above. Assertively contemporary in its effect, the colour scheme provides another counterpoint to the surviving elements of the original architecture.

The use of strong colour is allied with a programme of specially commissioned works of art, most of them for specific locations in the building. Together, they constitute one of Germany's most important contemporary public arts projects. The majority are by East and West German artists, but – in a further gesture of reconciliation – artists from the original

Four Powers also contributed (Foster himself was considered to be the English 'artist'). Together with the colour scheme, they provide a further layer of intervention in the historical palimpsest that the Reichstag represents. As Foster himself observes, 'the Reichstag is both a museum of memories and a gallery of contemporary art – within its walls a record of both the most tragic and the most uplifting aspects of Germany's cultural history are preserved for future generations.'

Unifying the entire building and all its activities both visually and symbolically and cutting through the alternating layers of parliamentary, public and semi-public space are the conjoined volumes of the cupola and the lofty assembly chamber, which form a 40-metre high, vertically transparent continuum from the floor of the chamber to the oculus of the dome.

As is usual in Foster's practice, the design of the cupola itself underwent rigorous development before arriving at its final form. During the final stages of the competition Foster came to believe that the renovated Reichstag needed a 'marker on the skyline' which would give external expression to the political and physical changes within: a structure that would function as a 'lantern', bringing light – both natural and symbolic – to the political proceedings below.

Above left: The Reichstag's combined heat and power generator, which burns refined vegetable oil, derived from rape or sunflower seeds.

Above right: The absorption cooling plant uses surplus heat energy to produce chilled water for summer cooling.

Seeing the Reichstag sparkling in its silver shroud and witnessing the extraordinary festival that sprang up around it was a magical experience.
Norman Foster, 2011

Above and top: In the summer of 1995, shortly before reconstruction work began, the moment of the Reichstag's rebirth was brilliantly captured by Christo and Jeanne-Claude's *Wrapped Reichstag*, a project first conceived by the artists in 1971.

In Foster's mind, however, that did not necessarily imply a dome, though neither did it exclude that possibility. Eventually the designers settled down to exploring two main alternatives: one a tall lattice structure, called the 'lighthouse'; the other, a more conventionally shaped cupola with a curtailed top.

Both structures, however, were also conceived as much more than lanterns, and like the earlier umbrella roof scheme, were fully integrated into the building's environmental systems. As part of this approach, the 'lighthouse' featured a saucer-like wind- and sun-scoop reminiscent of some of Foster's earlier works, intended to shelter the top of the structure and divert daylight and air movement downwards. Both schemes also included versions of the spiral ramps and mirrored cone, which are such distinctive features of the final design. Sweeping upwards to an observation platform, and then back down again to the roof (visitors move upwards in an anti-clockwise direction and downwards in a clockwise direction to avoid congestion) the twin ramps were designed to provide the public with unrivalled views across Berlin and also glimpses into the assembly chamber beneath.

Once the idea of the mirrored cone was accepted it was then developed with the lighting designer, Claude Engle, another regular collaborator with the Foster studio. Shaped to reflect daylight from the horizon deep into the chamber, the dual-purpose cone also functions as an exhaust system to draw out stale air from the chamber naturally through the stack effect. A typical product of Foster's exacting process of 'design development', a highly detailed 1:20-scale prototype – large enough for three people to stand inside – was tested acoustically and under real daylight conditions on the roof of the Reichstag to prove the scheme's effectiveness.

Only when Foster was convinced himself of the merits of the cupola over the alternative did he proceed with the final design. Comparing the two options, there can be no doubt the final choice was the correct one. For all its original features, the 'lighthouse' with its odd shape and 'saucer' on top, sat awkwardly on the Reichstag roof. The new dome, by contrast, with its simple and easily recognisable outline and structure, fits comfortably into place. Its circular shape and silhouette are far removed from the historical four-sided dome.

So this is no ordinary cupola. Hanging in the centre of the dome and sparkling like a great pendant, the multi-faceted cone could well be interpreted as 'the jewel in the crown' of the Reichstag. This regal and ambiguous image is, however, further complicated

and greatly enriched by many other, contrary images. Lightweight, totally transparent, publicly accessible and designed as much to save energy in the building as anything else; both in structure and multi-functional purpose, Foster's populated cupola effectively undermines any simplistic associations with hierarchical power or the like, despite its conventional placement. Suspended in space, men, women and children move freely up and down the ramps, their reflections in the cone's mirrors adding to the surreal effect. After dark, when the assembly chamber is in use, the cone reverses its function to reflect light into the night sky. On ceremonial occasions, twelve beams of light (the 'Twelve Apostles') are projected to spectacular effect from high-intensity xenon lamps, transforming the dome into a glowing beacon: a clear sign of activity to the watchful German electorate.

Backing up the dome's highly visible environmental systems is a battery of advanced techniques representing the state of the art in low-energy, sustainable design. Here Foster was able to capitalise directly on the practice's German experience. The three Duisburg buildings – the Business Promotion Centre, Microelectronic Centre and Telematic Forum – were nearing completion at the time of the Reichstag competition and were clearly influential. In Duisburg,

in association with Norbert Kaiser who became a consultant to the Reichstag project, the Foster team had developed the technology to reclaim the heat from extracted air and to convert warm water into cold, using an absorption cooling plant; they also explored ways of storing hot and cold water for future use – techniques that would be exploited here.

What Foster calls 'the energy story' was a powerful component of his presentation to the second-stage competition jury, which included members of the Building Committee and their technical advisors. He asked them an apparently simple question: 'how much does it cost to run the Reichstag?' He said he was sure they knew how much it cost to heat their own homes, but could they tell him how much they spent on their parliamentary home. As he suspected, nobody knew; but he had the answer ready. It cost approximately 2.5 million Deutschmarks annually to run the heating, lighting, air-conditioning and so forth.

Foster's team had calculated that the building consumed enough energy annually to heat 5,000 German homes; that its oil-fired heating boilers produced an astonishing 7,000 tonnes of carbon dioxide annually; and that raising the temperature by one degree on a winter's day required a burst of energy sufficient to heat ten houses for a year.

As Foster says, 'it was a dinosaur in terms of attitudes prevailing in Germany in the 1990s.'

Foster argued that, as representatives of the body that set standards of energy conservation and pollution for the nation, the German parliament had a responsibility to provide in the Reichstag a model for others to follow. But he also told his audience that it was possible to reduce running costs dramatically: 'so if they did not do it for moral reasons, then they should definitely do it for Deutschmarks.'

From being one of Berlin's largest single sources of airborne pollution, the Reichstag has been transformed into a model of responsible environmental behaviour, producing just 440 tonnes of carbon dioxide – a 94 per cent reduction. Power is generated by burning 'bio-diesel' – refined vegetable oil extracted from sunflower or rape seeds – in a co-generator. This provides a clean, efficient, renewable source of energy. As an illustration of how efficient the system is, if the Reichstag were to burn natural gas, the carbon dioxide figure would be in the region of 1,450 tonnes per annum – more than three times the amount. In practice, because its own energy requirements are sufficiently modest, the Reichstag produces more power than it needs, which means that it effectively performs as a local power station in the Spreebogen quarter.

Right above: The battle- and graffiti-scarred remains of Wallot's Reichstag interiors have a tremendous poignancy; in the east corridor, the cyclopean stones surrounding once elaborate doorways have an almost archaeological quality.

Right below: A sketch study by Norman Foster for the treatment of one of the newly reopened doorways in the east corridor.

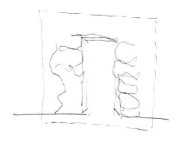

Right: Norman Foster, Mark Braun, and members of the Reichstag design team gathered in front of the building on 7 July 1995, the day that Christo's wrapping was taken down.

Using techniques borrowed from the oil-exploration industry, surplus waterborne heat emitted by the power plant during summer can be transferred to underground seasonal energy reservoirs. Heat is discharged as warm water down one of two boreholes into a natural aquifer located more than 300 metres below ground. In winter, the stored warm water is pumped back up into the building, via the second borehole, to provide supplementary heating via a network of under-floor pipes. Cold water is similarly pumped from a shallower aquifer, 60 metres underground, to cool the building via chilled ceilings in summer. (Surplus heat from the co-generator can also be recycled to produce chilled water using an absorption-cooling plant.)

Even the masonry fabric of the building is enlisted into the system. Removing the plaster linings from the 1960s, to expose the heavy structure behind, was a first step towards releasing the building's thermal potential. The energy conservation strategy relies on the building's thermal mass to maintain a comfortable base temperature from which active heating or cooling can provide 'topping up' as required. In this way, peak loads are reduced by as much as 30 per cent.

The environmental systems also take account of the different thermal properties of the various elements in the building. Spaces within the heavy masonry walls perform very differently from the rooms on the new third floor, for example. In the faction and committee rooms chilled ceilings ensure comfortable conditions under most scenarios. Only under extreme conditions – if a committee room is suddenly packed for a meeting – will air conditioning cut in temporarily to cope with the extra heat load.

Natural lighting and ventilation are also exploited as far as possible. The ducts that drew fresh air into Wallot's chamber were found to have survived and were put to new use. Fresh air – from what Foster calls the 'green lung' of the Tiergarten – is drawn in through a duct above the portico on the west side of the building and taken down into a large plenum below the chamber. From there it rises as low-velocity ventilation through the perforated mesh of the floor and the loose-weave carpet. The air moves slowly up through the space as it warms, is extracted at ceiling level and exhausted through a nozzle in the top of the cone; heat exchangers recover a proportion of the heat from the air before it is expelled. Air pressure within the chamber is monitored and the rate of extraction can be adjusted to ensure that a comfortable environment is maintained. The system works naturally, although the process can be mechanically assisted if required. At

Right: A Japanese 'masonry muncher' with a 43-metre boom, eats away at redundant concrete beams and columns; 45,000 tonnes of demolition materials were removed from the building over a period of four months.

roof level, photovoltaics power the moving sunscreen that tracks the path of the sun to control the amount of sunlight reflected into the chamber.

The significance of Foster's environmental scheme is underlined by the fact that at the development stage, the design team was awarded a grant under the European Commission's renewable energy programme – a project that subsequently became known as the 'Solar Reichstag'.

In the summer of 1995, while the detailed design of the building was being finalised, the moment of the Reichstag's rebirth was brilliantly captured by Christo and Jeanne-Claude's *Wrapped Reichstag*, a project first conceived by the artists in 1971. For two weeks in late June and early July the building in its silvery 'cocoon' was the centre of spontaneous public expression and festivities, drawing crowds of visitors as well as Berliners day and night to celebrate the coming transformation. As Foster remembers it, the extraordinary event seemed to have a cathartic effect '… it seemed to unburden the building of its more tragic associations and prepare it for the next phase of its career.'

The experience for this writer, returning to Berlin after an absence of nearly a quarter of a century and seeing the results of the Reichstag's transformation,

was not a little moving. It was not hard to imagine what the impact on Berliners themselves must be, not to mention the rest of the millions of visitors (3.5 million in the first year alone) who have flocked to the Reichstag since its completion. Ascending the ramp inside the cupola to the observation platform and looking out over the forest of cranes crowding the changing skyline towards the East, there was a palpable sense of participating in a historical process of immense dimensions, which the Reichstag in its reincarnation had helped to crystallise.

Perhaps the most poignant moment though, was seeing the graffiti inscribed on the Reichstag's walls by those eager Russian soldiers in their final moment of triumph, now revealed for all to see again: pages in a unique 'notebook of history', as Foster intended, not without their own pain for many who will have read them. A courageous decision on the part of all of those involved, architects and politicians alike, their exposure and preservation is an apt and powerful reminder, as the Reichstag itself is, that 'democracy is a fragile good, easily lost'.[1]

1. Wilhelm Vossenkuhl, 'The Reichstag: Metamorphosis' in *Rebuilding the Reichstag*, 2000

Opposite left and right: In July 1995 demolition work commenced. The process involved stripping the building of the structural interventions made in the 1960s while preserving what little remained of the nineteenth-century interiors.

Above left: An aerial view of the Reichstag under construction on 1 February 1997; the form of the new chamber can be seen taking shape.

Above right: A little under six months later, on 23 July, the ramps within the cupola are beginning to rise.

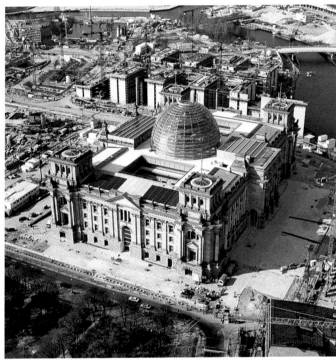

Above left: By 24 March 1998 the external form of the cupola can be appreciated, though it has yet to be glazed.

Above right: In this photograph, taken on 1 April 1999 – a few weeks before the opening ceremony – the building is practically complete and external works are under way.

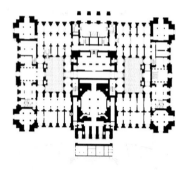

1894

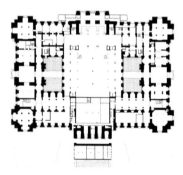

1971

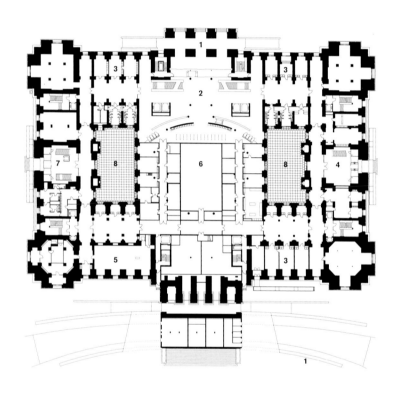

1999

Plan at ground level and comparative plans as completed by Wallot and Baumgarten in 1894 and 1971 respectively. Baumgarten cut corridors through the courtyards and displaced the building's main entrance to the south at this level.

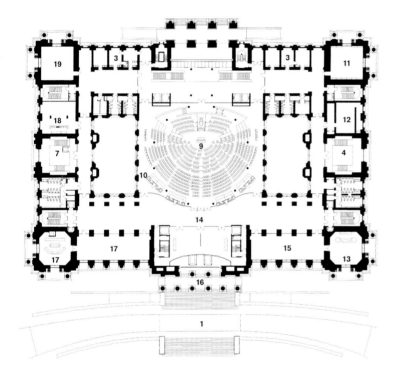

1894

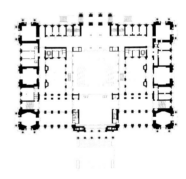

1971

1999

Plan at first floor level, the principal parliamentary floor, with comparative plans by Wallot and Baumgarten. Wallot's chamber was far smaller and displaced to the east behind an octagonal entrance hall. Baumgarten oriented his chamber so that the speaker faced east.

1 driveway
2 east entrance lobby
3 offices
4 south entrance lobby
5 kitchen
6 plant rooms
7 north entrance lobby
8 courtyards
9 plenary chamber
10 translators' cabins

11 function room
12 chapel
13 club room
14 west lobby
15 lobby
16 public entrance
17 MPs' restaurant
18 cafeteria
19 library

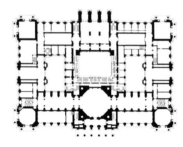

1894

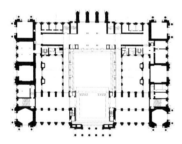

1971

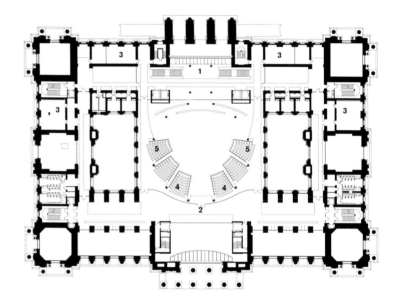

1999

Previous pages: The Reichstag
seen from the west.

Above: Plan at mezzanine level,
from where the public has access
to the tribunes in the chamber,
and comparative plans as
completed by Wallot and
Baumgarten in 1894 and
1971 respectively.

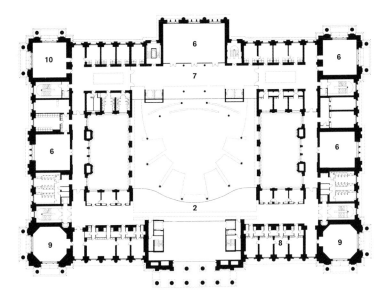

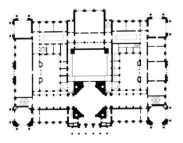

1894

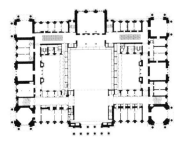

1971

1999

Plan at second floor level, largely
the preserve of the President of
the Bundestag and parliamentary
administration, and comparative
plans as completed by Wallot
and Baumgarten.

1 east bridge
2 west bridge
3 lecture rooms
4 press tribunes
5 public tribunes
6 function room
7 east lobby
8 offices
9 meeting room
10 Council of Elders

Above: Visitors queue for admission on the steps of the Reichstag – a familiar scene in the daily life of the building.

Right: New and old juxtaposed; within the cupola a steady stream of visitors ascends to the viewing platform.

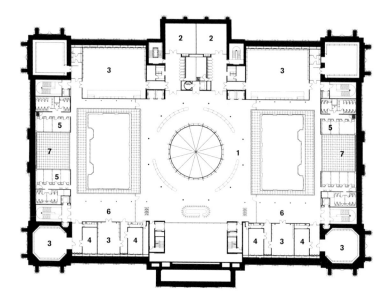

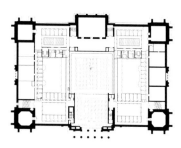

1971

1999

Plan at third floor level, a new
floor housing faction rooms
and the press lobby, and a
comparative plan as completed
by Baumgarten in 1971; there
was no equivalent floor level in
the nineteenth-century building.

0   20m

0   60ft

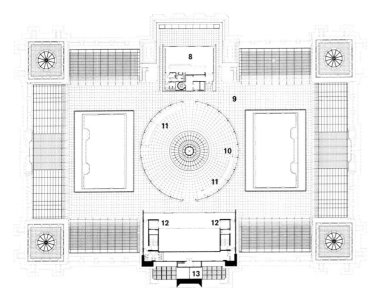

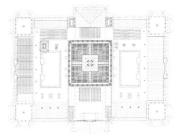

1894

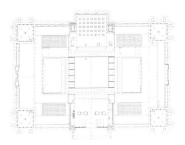

1971

1999

Plan at roof level, the building's principal public level, with comparative plans as completed by Wallot and Baumgarten. In Wallot's scheme the roof level was inaccessible; in Baumgarten's reconstruction light-wells served a new floor of offices.

1 press lobby
2 party lobby
3 party meeting rooms
4 party boardrooms
5 offices
6 lobby
7 terrace
8 roof café
9 public roof terrace

10 cupola
11 ramps to viewing platform
12 public lifts to west lobby
13 plant

Left: Approached through the
West Portico at night, the building
becomes transparent, revealing
the volume of the chamber.

Above: Looking into the west
entrance hall with its monumental
German flag, executed in glass
by Gerhard Richter.

Above: Looking down through the West Portico from the press lobby on the third floor

Right: Standing in the west entrance hall, looking into the chamber; arriving visitors have a clear view of the seats of the Chancellor, the President of the Bundestag and other national leaders.

Overleaf: A view into the chamber
from mezzanine level in the
west lobby.

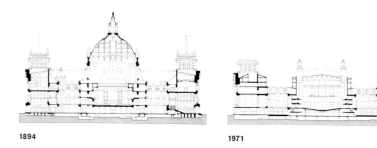

1894

1971

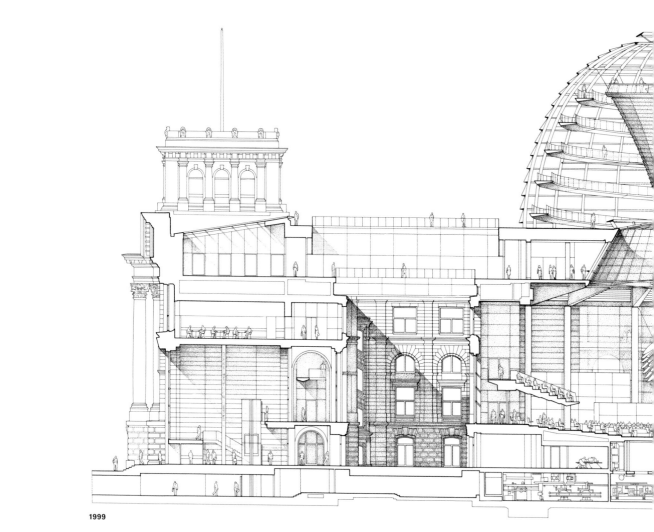

1999

0   10m

0   30ft

A north-south cross-section
through the chamber, looking
towards the seat of the
President of the Bundestag,
and comparative sections
as completed by Wallot and
Baumgarten in 1894 and
1971 respectively.

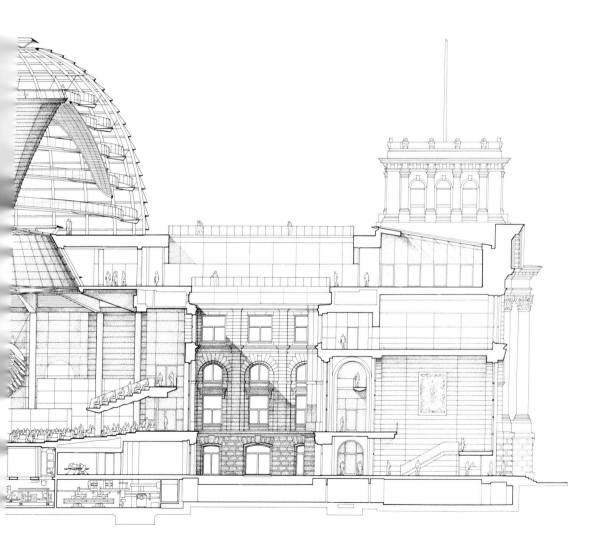

The new parliamentary chamber – its form set in spatial harmony with the cupola above … offers a new vision of democracy, the impact of which is felt both within the Reichstag and without.
Rita Süssmuth, former President of the Bundestag, *Rebuilding the Reichstag*, 2000

Above: Looking across the chamber from a vantage point in the public tribunes.

Right: A bird's-eye view of the chamber and the 'bicycle-wheel' bracing of the cone, as seen from the press lobby on the third floor.

Trendelkamp
nr. Münster
15-6-98
mark by Rudi M.

Left: The Reichstag eagle seen from the east lobby. When in September 1996 the German parliament decided to retain the Bonn eagle, designed by Ludwig Gies, it fell to Norman Foster to reinvent it to work sculpturally in three dimensions.

Above: Design sketches of the eagle by Norman Foster, including those drawn on a visit to the Trendelkamp workshops, where the eagle was made.

Above: Günther Uecker's multi-faith chapel on the first floor represents perhaps the most complete interaction between art and architecture in the Reichstag. In collaboration with Uecker, the room's layout and finishes were specified to reinforce his overall vision.

Right: The first-floor members' lobby contains a work by Katharina Sieverding which commemorates members of the Reichstag murdered or persecuted by the Nazis.

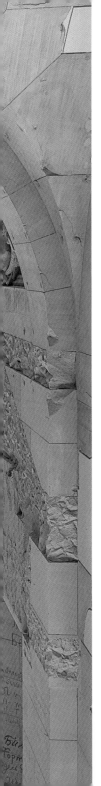

Each age produces its own vocabulary, has its own integrity and makes its own mark ... How you bring the old and the new together is an approach which has been quite fundamental to the thinking of our practice.
Norman Foster, 2011

Left: The north corridor is among the best preserved of Wallot's spaces. The walls and niches carry the scars of war – broken stones and Russian graffiti – but also those from the 1960s when the ornamental carving was chiselled away. Steel bridges at mezzanine level allow access to the public tribunes.

Above: The east corridor, which runs into the east lobby, is a legacy of Baumgarten's interventions. But whereas Baumgarten divided the space horizontally, it has been opened up so that the space rises through three levels.

An example of the Russian
graffiti preserved in the east
corridor. Throughout the building,
where new work meets old
the junction has been articulated,
allowing each layer in the
building's complex history
to be read clearly.

It is clear that for many Russians the Reichstag was symbolically the closest thing in Berlin to the Kremlin in Moscow. To write on its walls was therefore the ultimate taboo, the final statement of victory. Frederick Baker, *The Reichstag Graffiti*, 2002

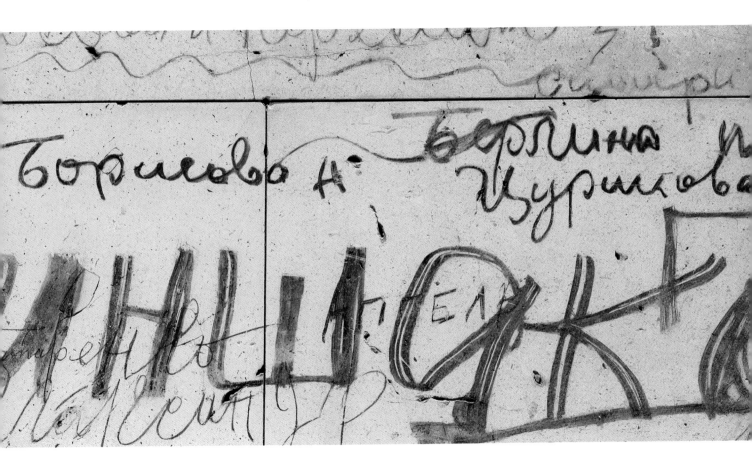

In its new incarnation, the Reichstag wears the scars of history bravely ... It embodies memories of terrible things, and yet with its transparency and multi-layered thoughtfulness, it offers hope. Peter Davey, *The Architectural Review*, July 1999

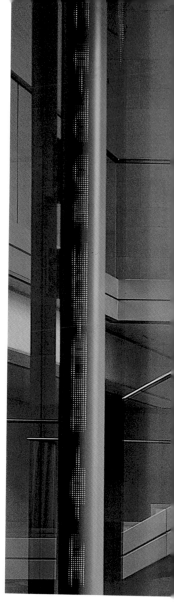

Left: New staircases occupy the nineteenth-century stairwells. Paul Wallot's ornate stairs survived the war but were swept away during the 1960s' rebuilding, when floor levels in the building were changed.

Above: The north entrance lobby, which occupies the shell of Wallot's original space, contains an installation by the American artist Jenny Holzer, whose digital light system quotes from speeches that have helped to frame German democracy.

Left: The southern courtyard
contains a stone relief sculpture
by Ulrich Rückriem.

Above: A view of the north
courtyard; the courtyards survive
from Paul Wallot's nineteenth-
century Reichstag and once
again form major organising
elements in the plan.

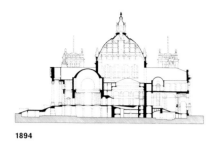

1894

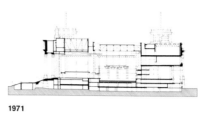

1971

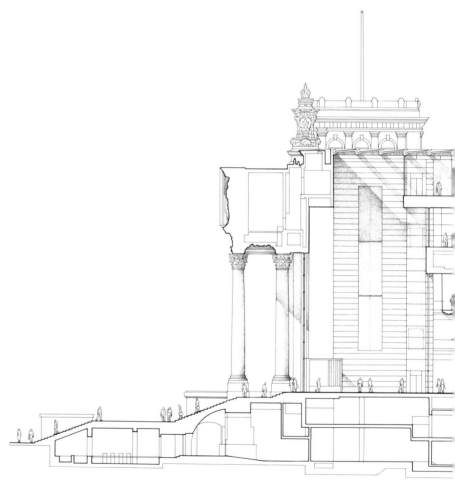

1999

An east-west cross-section through the chamber and comparative sections as completed by Wallot and Baumgarten in 1894 and 1971 respectively. Wallot's entry sequence from the west has been reinstated, as has the principal parliamentary level, or piano nobile. The horizontal stratification of Baumgarten's rebuilding has been swept away: the new chamber and cupola together provide a strong vertical emphasis.

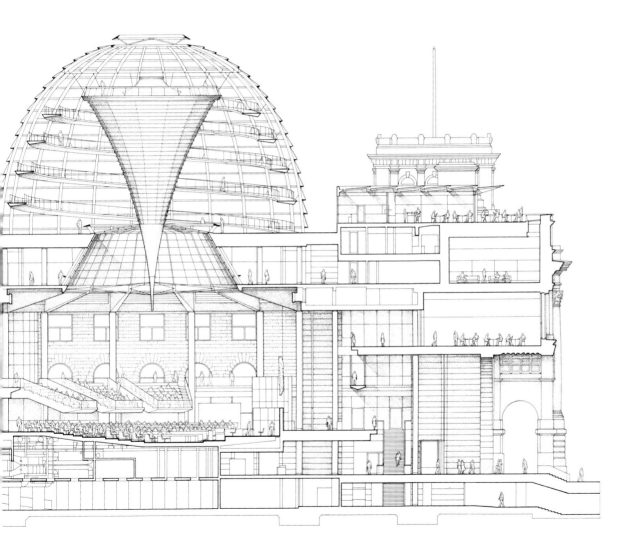

The building's tour de force is the dome ... It has already become the city's new icon, visible everywhere among the skyline of new glass and metal office towers and the dour domes and spires of the imperial past.
James S Russell, *Architectural Record*, July 1999

Previous pages: People on the roof terrace and the ramps of the new cupola: it is here that the contrast between the heaviness of the old fabric and the lightness of the new is most pronounced.

Left and above: Some 2.7 million people visit the Reichstag every year. Within the cupola, hushed voices are carried across the space as they might be in the whispering gallery of a cathedral dome.

It was fascinating to watch the mirrored cone in the heart of the cupola grow from a vague technical idea, pass through all its development stages, and emerge as something that has a profound symbolic meaning; that was very special. David Nelson, of Foster + Partners, 2011

Looking up through the louvred
sunshade that moves on rails
around the inside of the cupola
to track the path of the sun
and block solar gain and glare.

Above and right: Throughout the year, not just on public holidays, the Reichstag's roof terrace and cupola are among Berlin's major visitor attractions.

Above: The public restaurant at roof level has also become a popular lunch venue for members of parliament.

Right: The restaurant terrace, which has since been enclosed, enjoys one of the best views in Berlin across to the Brandenburg Gate and the city centre.

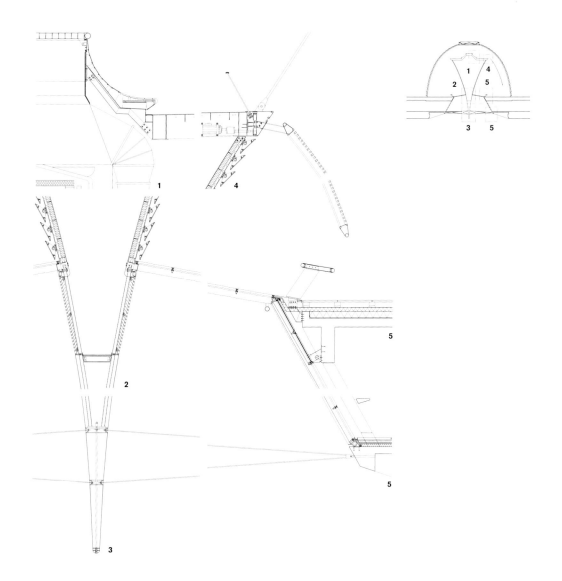

Left: A detail of the cupola's faceted glazing.

Above: Details of the mirrored cone and glazed chamber soffit.

1 section at viewing platform level
2 section at chamber soffit level
3 detail of the 'bicycle-wheel' bracing
4 section through the sunshade
5 detail of the press lobby glazing

Overleaf: At night the cupola becomes a beacon on the Berlin skyline.

Facts and figures

New German Parliament, Reichstag

Berlin, Germany
1992-1999
Client
Bundesrepublik Deutschland
Project Team
Norman Foster
David Nelson
Mark Braun
Stefan Behling
Ulrich Hamann
Christian Hallmann
Dieter Müller
Ingo Pott

Chris Allerkamp
Nick Baker
John Ball
Alexander Barry
Simon Beames
Serge Belet
Susanne Bellinghausen
Etienne Borgos
Giuseppe Boscherini
Simon Bowden
Arthur Branthwaite
George Brennan
Caroline Brown
Hing Chan
Kei-Lu Cheong
Charles Collett
John Drew
Matteo Fantoni
Anja Flesch

Frank Glaesener
Ulrich Goertz
Helen Goodland
Nigel Greenhill
Tanya Griffiths
Pedro Haberbosch
Brandon Haw
Andreas Hell
Wendelin Hinsch
Robert Hoh
Alison Holroyd
William Hunt
Ken Hutt
Martin Hyams
Nadi Jahangiri
Ian Lomas
Andrea Ludwig
Alan Marten
David McDowell
Max Neal
Robin Partington
Simon Peckham
Nicola Pipe
Jan Roth
Paul Scott
Rupert Sherwood
Ken Shuttleworth
John Small
Kai Strehl
Henning Stummel
Mark Sutcliffe
Huw Turner
Ruggero Venelli
Juan Vieira-Pardo
Ken Wai

Robert Watson
Rolf Wiethege
Consultants
Acoustics: Müller BBM GmbH/Prof Dr Georg Plenge
Building Physics: Bobran Ingenieur
Cladding Consultant: Emmer Pfenninger Partner AG
Colour Consultant: Per Arnoldi
Conservation Consultant: Acanthus
Cost Consultant: Davis Langdon & Everest/Büro Am Lützowplatz
Lighting: Claude and Danielle Engle Lighting
Lifts, Materials, Handling Technology: Jappsen & Stangier
Mechanical, Electrical and Environmental Services: Kaiser Bautechnik/Fischer Energie & Haustechnik/Amstein & Walthert/Planungsgruppe Karnasch-Hackstein/Kuehn Associates
Structural Engineer: Arup/Schlaich Bergermann & Partner/Leonhardt, Andrä & Partner
Principal Awards
1999 Eurosol Preis für Solares Bauen
1999 RIBA Conservation Category Award
1999 RIBA Regional Architecture Award
1999 ECCS European Award for Steel Structures

1999 Deutscher Architekturpreis
1999 Architects' Journal and Bovis Europe Grand Award for Architecture at the Royal Academy Summer Exhibition
1999 Design Council Millennium Product Award
2000 Architekturpreis des BDA Berlin Auszeichnung
2000 Preis Des Deutschen Stahlbaues

Project chronology

1882 A competition is held for the design of the Reichstag; the Frankfurt architect Paul Wallot is the winner

1884 9 June: the foundation stone is laid by Kaiser Wilhelm I

1894 5 December: Kaiser Wilhelm II performs the topping out ceremony

1900 The Reichstag's interior decoration is completed

1916 December: the inscription Dem Deutschen Volke is unveiled on the Reichstag's West Portico

1918 9 November: Kaiser Wilhelm II abdicates; Social Democrat leader Philipp Scheidemann declares a German republic from a Reichstag balcony

1932 31 July: the Nazis win 230 Reichstag seats in new national elections, becoming the largest political party in Germany

1933 30 January: Adolf Hitler becomes Chancellor of Germany
27 February: the Reichstag chamber is destroyed by fire; a Dutch 'vagrant', Marinus van der Lubbe, is arrested

1945 30 April: Red Army troops attack the Reichstag
1 May: the Red Flag is raised above the East Portico
8 May: Field Marshal Keitel signs Germany's act of capitulation
5 July: Germany is divided into American, French, Soviet and British occupation zones; Berlin is located in the Soviet zone, but administered by the Four Powers; the Reichstag lies in the British sector

1949 23 May: the western zones of Germany become the Federal Republic of Germany
7 October: the Soviet zone of Germany becomes the German Democratic Republic

1955 The Bundestag debates the question of the rebuilding of the Reichstag and founds the Bundesbaudirektion (BBD) to address the issue

1960 A limited competition is held, in which ten architects are asked to submit proposals for the restoration of the Reichstag

1961 January: Paul Baumgarten is commissioned to rebuild the Reichstag
13 August: the Berlin Wall is erected

1971 21 March: the rebuilt Reichstag is opened, exactly 100 years after the establishment of the imperial parliament

1972 Christo makes his first collage for Wrapped Reichstag, Project for Berlin

1989 9 November: East Germans are allowed to cross into West Germany with immediate effect; the Berlin Wall is breached

1990 31 August: the Unification Treaty between the Federal Republic of Germany and the German Democratic Republic is finalised
3 October: Germany is formally reunified with Berlin as its capital
20 December: The united German parliament opens the Twelfth Legislative Period of the Bundestag in the Reichstag

1991 20 June: the German parliament narrowly votes for Berlin as the future seat of government
30 October: the Council of Elders votes to restore the Reichstag as the seat of parliament

1992 22 April: a competition is announced; it is open to

all German architects; fourteen international architects are also invited: Pi de Bruijn (the Netherlands), Santiago Calatrava (Switzerland), Dissing & Weitling (Denmark), Norman Foster (UK), Coop Himmelb(l)au (Austria), Hans Hollein (Austria), Helmut Jahn (USA), Juha Leiviskä (Finland), Fumihiko Maki (Japan), José Rafael Moneo (Spain), Jean Nouvel (France), I M Pei (USA), Aldo Rossi (Italy), Jiri Suchomel (CSFR)
The brief calls for 33,039 square metres of space – almost twice the area of the existing Reichstag building
31 July: the first Reichstag colloquium is held
23 October: 86 entries are submitted
31 October: the Bundestag moves into Günter Behnisch's parliament building in Bonn

1993 7-8 January: the first session of the Reichstag competition jury meets
27-29 January: a second session of the Reichstag competition jury votes to award first prize jointly to Pi de Bruijn, Santiago Calatrava and Norman Foster; Foster receives 75 per

cent of the vote, but the competition rules require a unanimous vote to win outright
19 February: the results of the competition are announced
12-13 March: the second Reichstag colloquium
25 March: the Council of Elders decides that there should be a second stage to the competition
29 April: the three winners are asked to revise their schemes to suit a more modest brief; the floor area is reduced to 9-12,000 square metres
22 June: the Building Committee meets to judge the revised proposals; Foster receives 16 of the 18 votes cast, De Bruijn receives two and Calatrava none; Foster is declared the winner
9 September: Foster is asked to produce a 'dome study'
10 September: the Bundesbaugesellschaft Berlin (BBB) is established to oversee construction of the new buildings in the Spreebogen area

1994 14 January: the German government allocates DM20 billion to move parliament, government and the civil service to Berlin
January: Foster produces

options for a feature rising above the Reichstag roof level; the preferred option is known as the 'lighthouse'
February: a budget of DM600 million is established for the conversion of the Reichstag, requiring cost reductions of approximately 10 per cent
25 February: the Bundestag approves proposals by Christo and Jeanne-Claude to wrap the Reichstag
28 April: the Building Committee asks Foster to produce a 'modern dome'
16 June: Foster presents two alternatives for a structure at roof level: the 'lighthouse' and a cupola with a truncated top

1995 2 February: Foster presents a new cupola design fully rounded at the top
9 March: the Bundestag votes in favour of the 'rounded-up' dome
24 June – 6 July: *Wrapped Reichstag* sparks a two-week popular festival in Berlin
7 July: demolition work begins

1996 28 February: Norman Foster is asked to design the eagle for the Reichstag chamber
13 March: construction of the steel and concrete primary

structure begins

December: meetings of the Parliamentary Art Committee are established to begin commissioning artists for the Reichstag

1997 May: general steel and concrete works are completed
June: construction of the cupola begins
18 September: a 'topping out' ceremony is held; the building is opened to the public and receives 60,000 visitors
26 September: the first test of the night-time illumination of the cupola is staged

1999 19 April: the Reichstag building is officially handed over; Norman Foster presents a symbolic key to the President of the Bundestag, Wolfgang Thierse; the first session of the house begins at 12.00 noon
21-25 April: public open days; over 150,000 people visit the Reichstag
26 April: the roof terrace and restaurant are opened to the public
8 September: the Bundestag commences regular plenary sessions in the Reichstag

Vital statistics

Visitor numbers
    2.7 million annually
Total cost
    600 million DM
Gross area
    61,166 square metres
Net area
    11,200 square metres
Diameter of cupola
    40 metres
Height of cupola
    23.5 metres
Height of observation platform above ground level
    40.7 metres
Total weight of cupola
    1,200 tonnes
Weight of cupola steelwork
    700 tonnes
Width of ramps within the cupola
    1.6 metres clear
Number of seats in the chamber
    750 – one for every MP, arranged according to party groupings
Light sculptor
    Covered with 360 polished mirrors, it weighs 300 tonnes and measures 2.5 metres in diameter, where it punctures the chamber ceiling, widening to 16 metres at the top

Environmental systems

The chamber is naturally ventilated; fresh air is drawn up through the space and out through the cone via the chimney effect

Heat exchangers recover and reutilise warm air not expelled through the dome

'Intelligent windows' comprise a manually operated inner layer and a security-laminated outer layer; fresh air is drawn in via ventilation joints

Renewable vegetable biofuel is burned in a co-generator to produce clean electricity, reducing annual carbon dioxide emissions by 94 per cent

Surplus heat is stored in a deep natural aquifer to provide hot water for heating

Cold water is stored below ground to provide cooling via chilled ceilings

Photovoltaic cells cover 300 square metres on the southern part of the roof

The Reichstag produces more electricity than it needs, effectively becoming a local power station in the new government quarter.

Credits

Editor: David Jenkins
Design: Thomas Manss
& Company; Thomas Manss,
Tom Featherby
Picture Research: Gayle Mault,
Lauren Catten
Proofreading: Julia Dawson,
Rebecca Roke
Production Supervision:
Martin Lee
Reproduction: Dawkins Colour
Printed and bound in Italy
by Grafiche SiZ S.p.A.

The FSC®-certified paper
GardaMatt has been supplied
by Cartiere del Garda S.p.A., Italy

Picture credits

Photographs
AKG Images: 17 (top right)
Bildarchiv Preussischer
Kulturbesitz: 18 (bottom)
Richard Bryant/Arcaid: 60, 62,
64, 86
Foster + Partners: 14, 15
(bottom), 22 (top, bottom right),
23 (top), 24, 28, 29 (top left), 30,
31, 33, 34 (bottom), 37 (top), 48,
52, 54, 56-57
Dennis Gilbert/VIEW: 49, 55, 61,
67, 76-77, 80-81, 84
Reinhard Görner: 44-45
Hulton Archive: 18 (top)
Landesbildstelle Berlin: 17 (top
left), 20, 21 (bottom left, bottom
right)
Novosti (London): 19 (top), 36
(top)
Rudi Meisel: 6-7, 29 (top right),
34 (top), 35, 36 (bottom left,
bottom right), 38, 39, 78, 82
Oltmann Reuter: 40, 41
Soviet Group/Magnum Photos:
19 (bottom)
Ullsteinbild/Günther Schneider:
21 (top)
Nigel Young/Foster + Partners:
26 (bottom left, bottom middle,
bottom right), 27 (bottom left,
bottom middle, bottom right), 37
(bottom), 53, 65, 66, 68-69, 70,
71, 72, 73, 79, 83, 85, 88-89,
94-95

Drawings and Sketches
Birds Portchmouth Russum:
74-75
Das Reichstagsgebäude in
Berlin, Cosmos Verlag, Leipzig
1897: 16
Norman Foster: 4, 5, 22 (bottom
left), 23 (bottom), 63, 74 (top left,
top right)

Foster + Partners: 25, 26 (top
left, top right); 32, 42, 43, 46, 47,
50, 51, 58-59, 87
Gregory Gibbon: 12-13

Every effort has been made
to contact copyright holders.
The publishers apologise for
any omissions which they
will be pleased to rectify at
the earliest opportunity.

Editor's Note

In editing this book I am
particularly grateful to Norman
Foster and Chris Abel for their
invaluable contributions. I would
also like to thank Thomas
Manss and Tom Featherby for
bringing the book to life
graphically; Gayle Mault and
Lauren Catten, who mined the
office archive; Julia Dawson and
Rebecca Roke for proofreading
the text; John Bodkin and Martin
Lee for coordinating production;
and the numerous people in the
Foster studio – past and present
– who helped piece together
the background to the project.

David Jenkins
London, July 2011